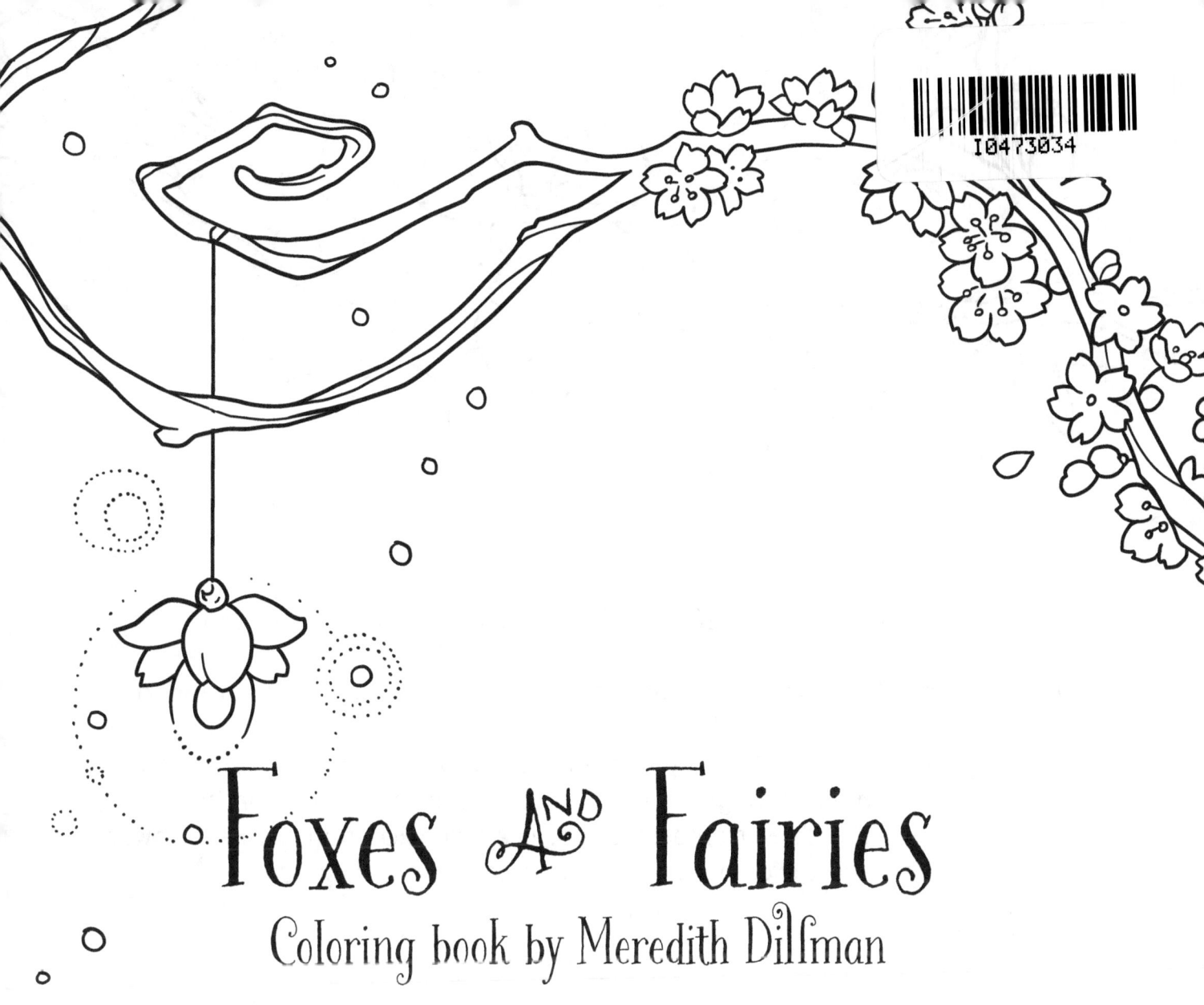

Foxes And Fairies

Coloring book by Meredith Dillman

This book is a collection of my illustrations inspired by Japanese, Chinese and Korean fox spirit myths, traditional costumes and nature. I have chosen these images from artwork spanning over 10 years of my career (so there are some differences in style over time). I drew inspiration from my time studying in Japan during college, manga, ukiyo-e prints and traditional paintings combined with my love of fantasy and fairies. Character costumes include traditional kimonos to fantastical takes on kimono, hanfu, and hanbok. Each artwork is based one of my finished ink and watercolor paintings. I hope you will enjoy bringing them to life by adding color!

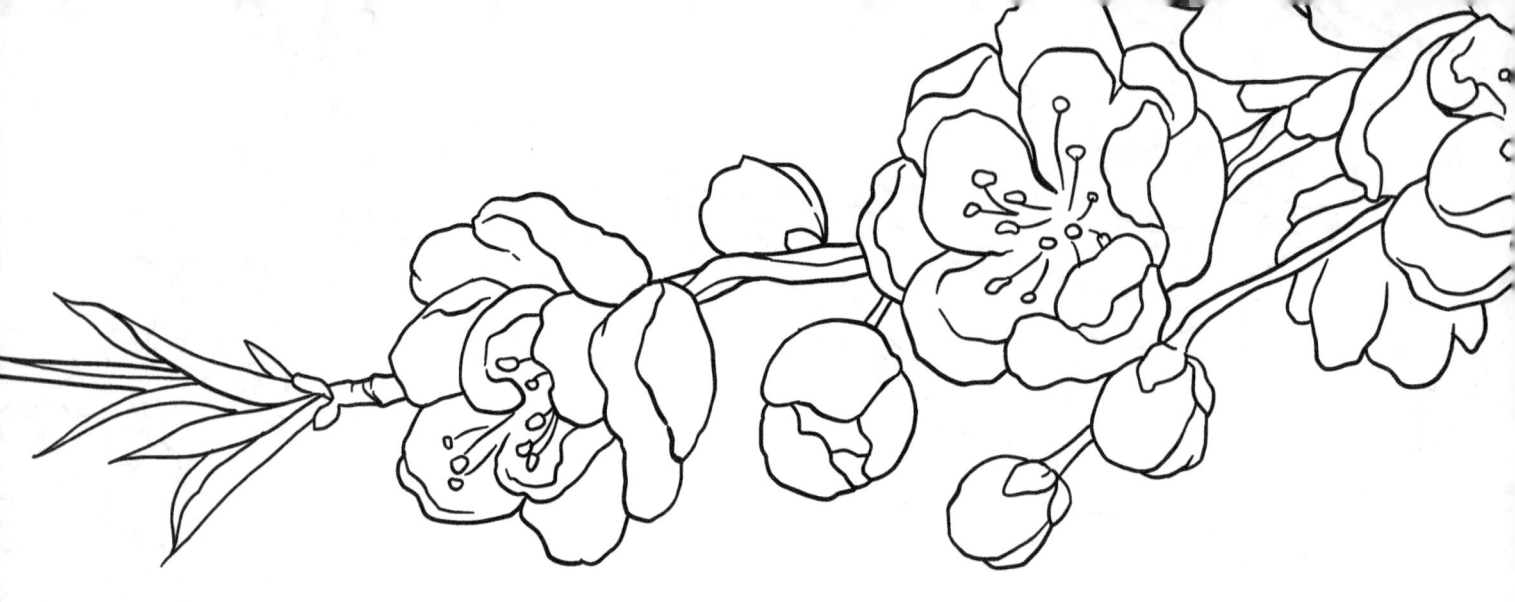

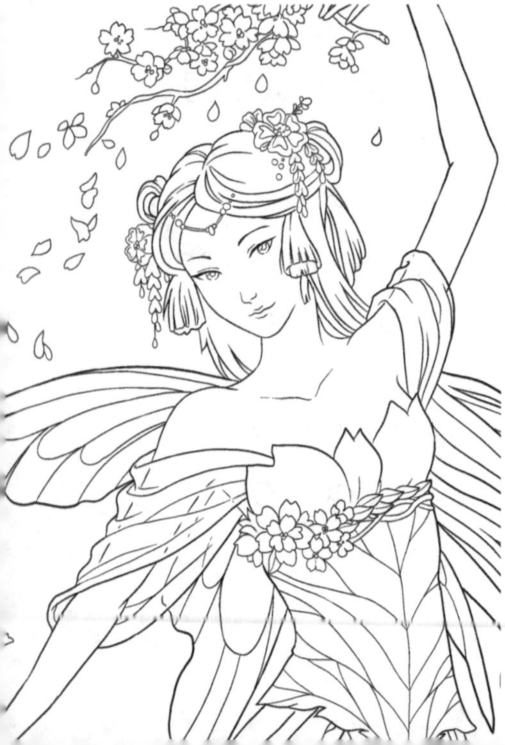

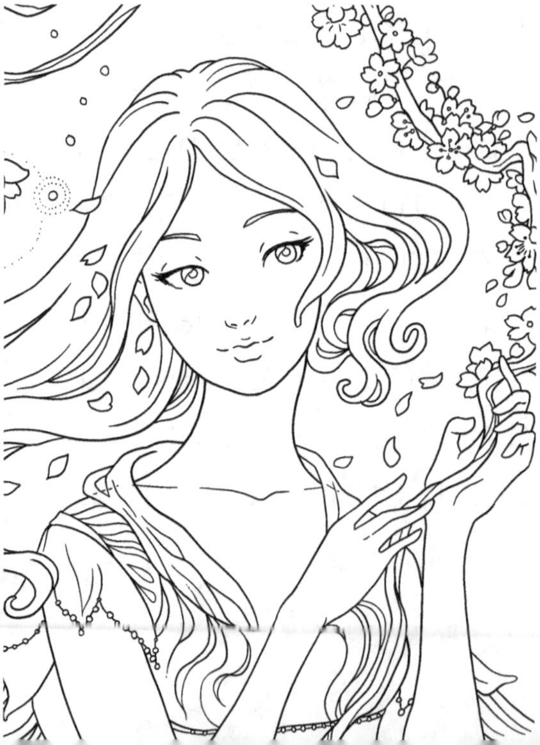

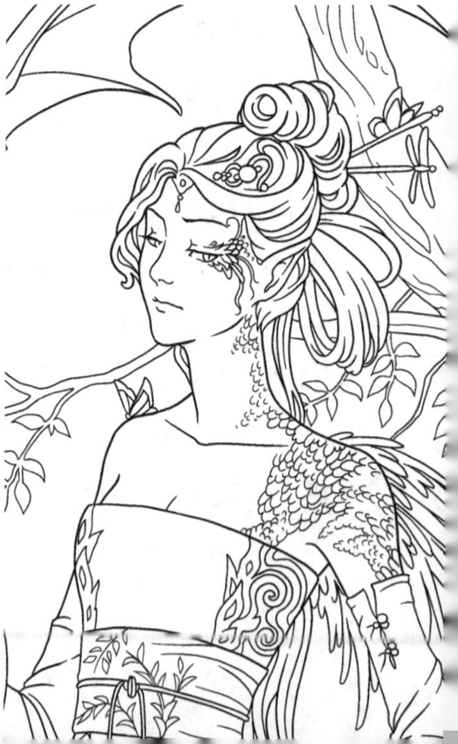

How to use this book

• Use color pencils, markers or a combination with this book. Gel pens and glitter pens make great accents too.

• Images are printed on one side only. The paper is not bleed proof so please place a heavy piece of paper or few sheets of copy paper under each page to avoid bleed through or indentations on other pages.

• Most importantly, have fun and relax! Enjoy bringing each image to life with your own color choices. Remember no color combination is wrong and experimentation is fine. Nothing in art needs to be the color we expect it to be in real life.

• If you post your colored versions online please credit Meredith Dillman and link to meredithdillman.com - Thank you!

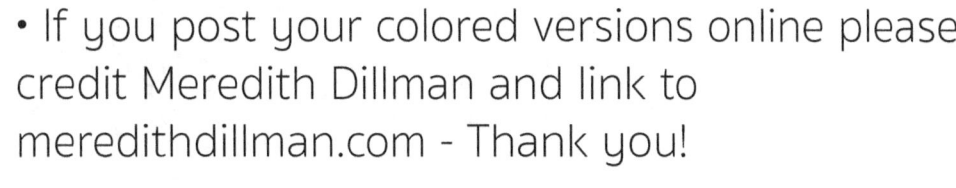

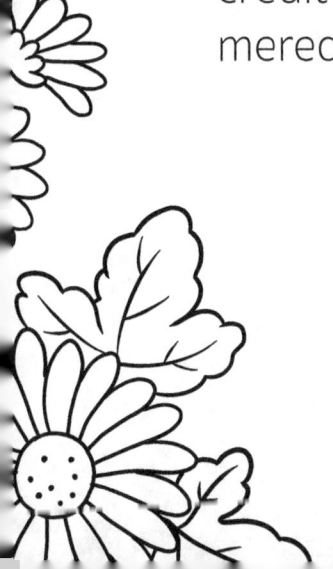

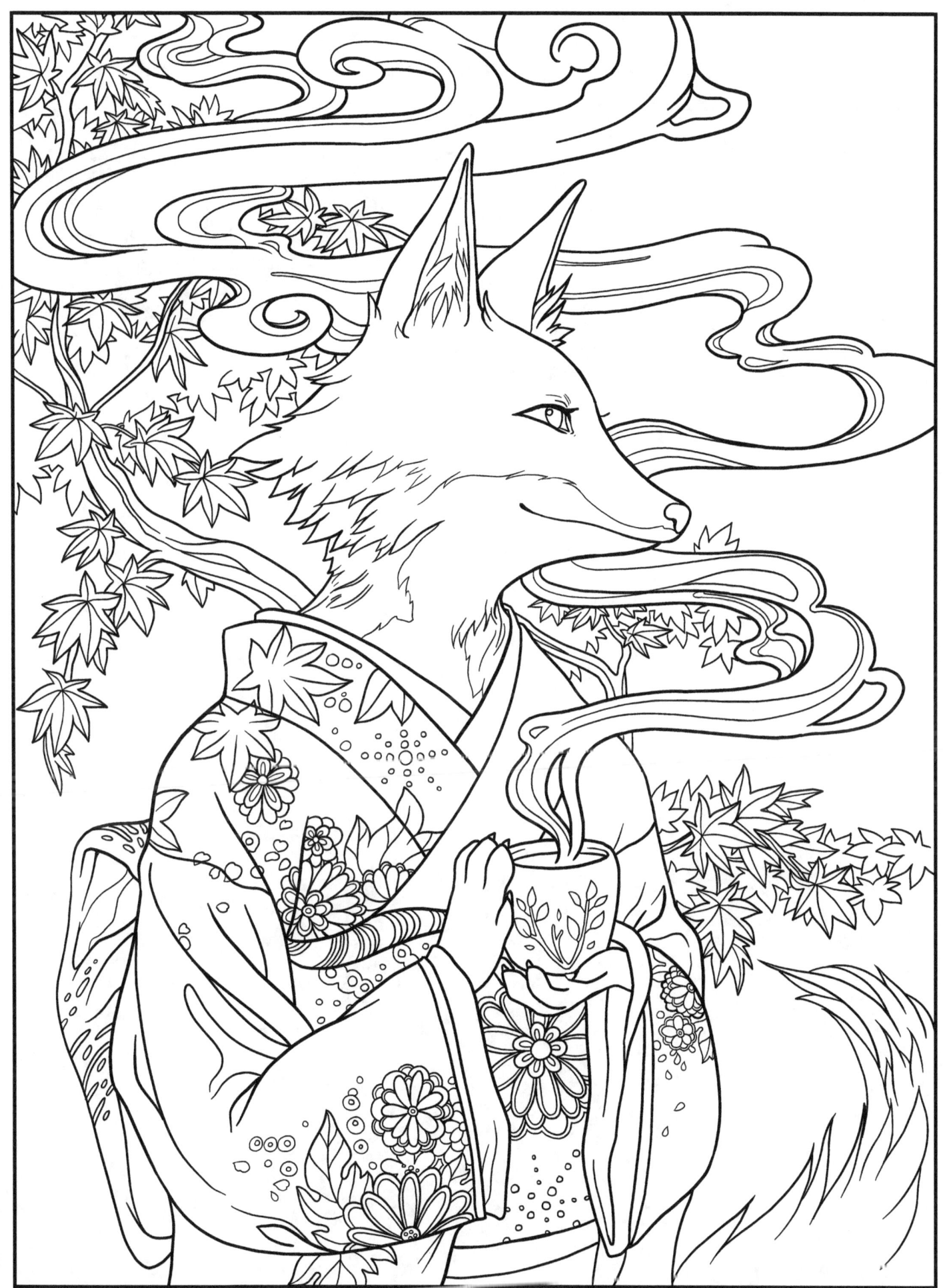

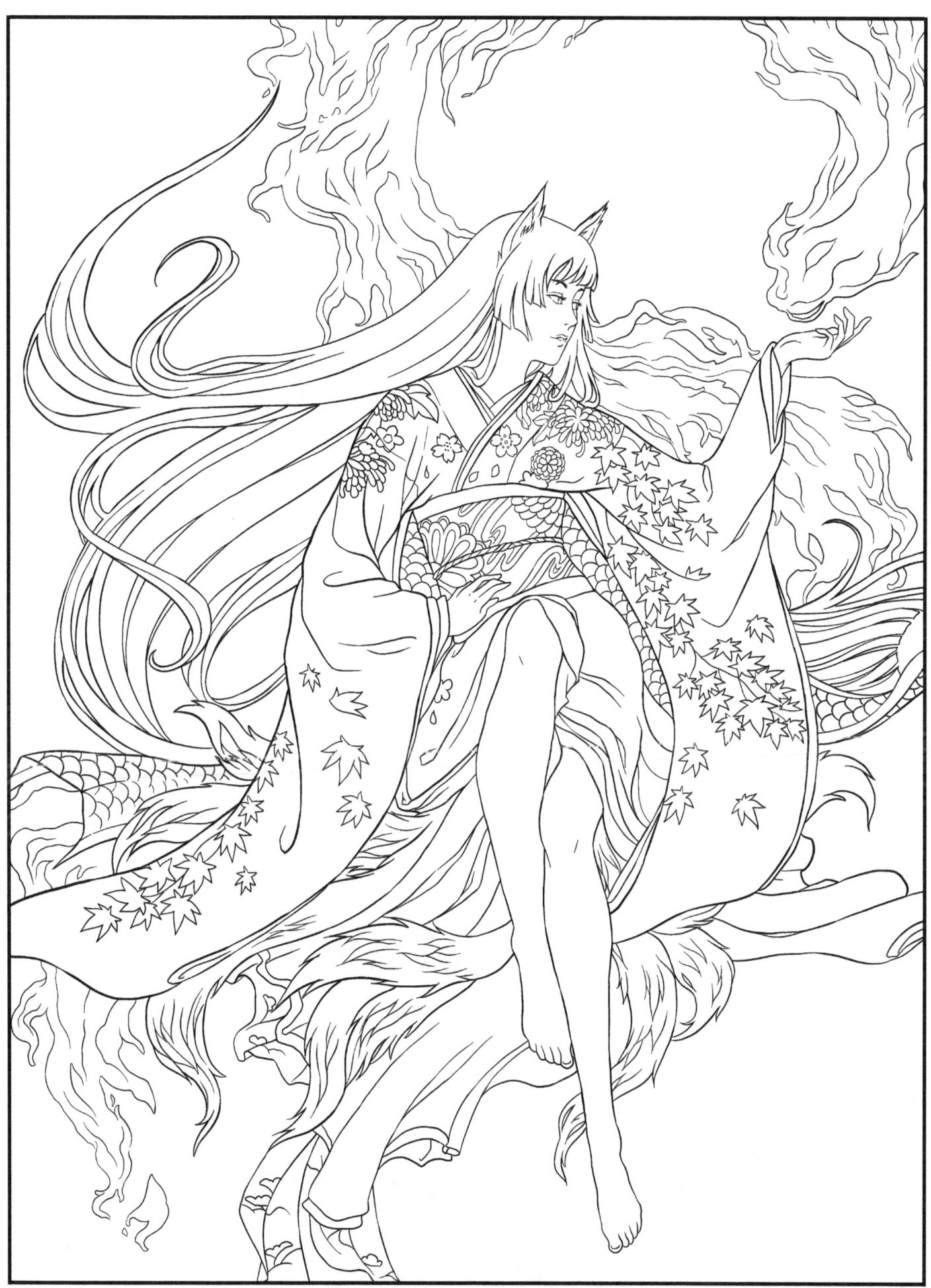

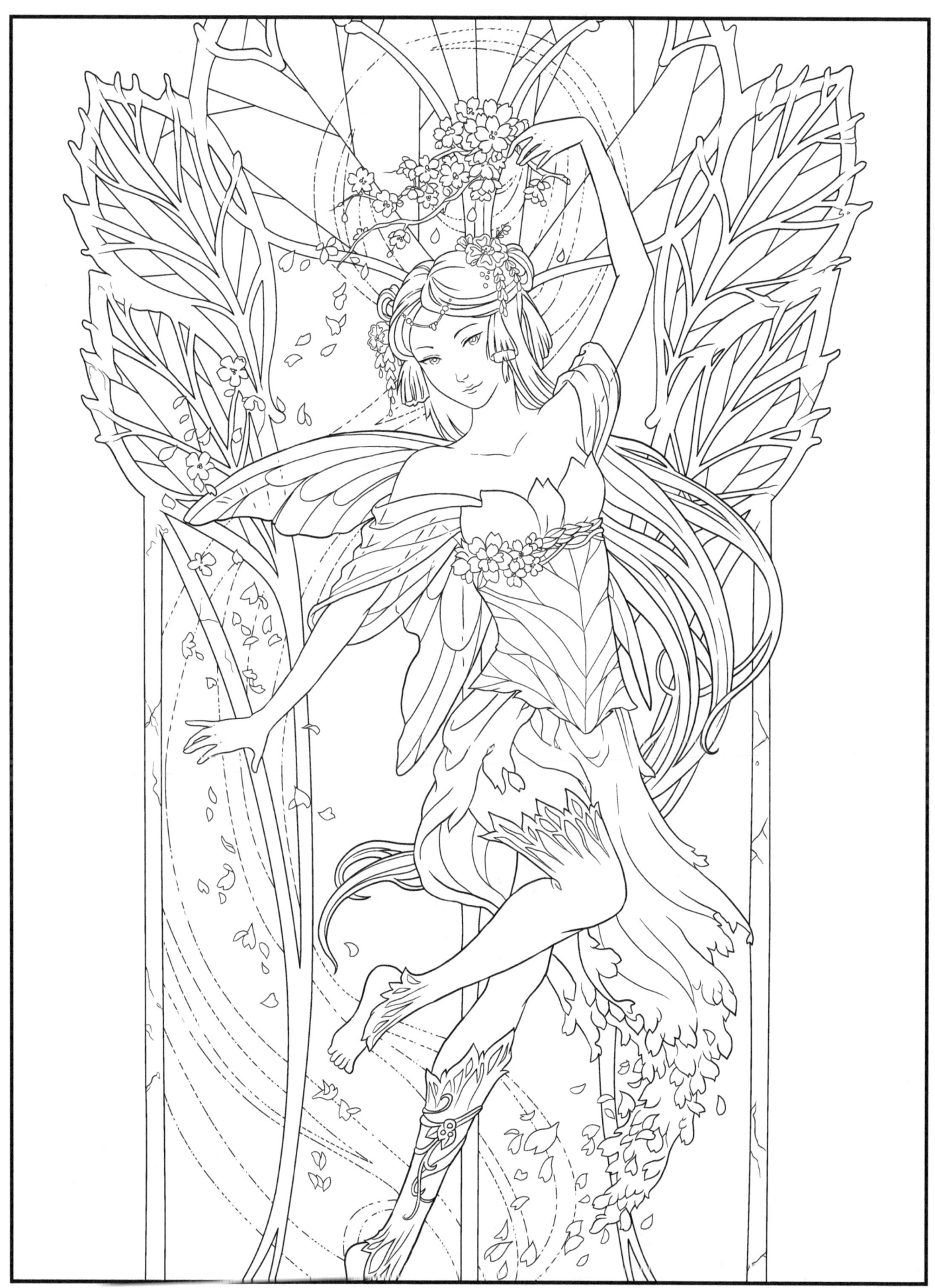

Previous Page: Blossoming Spring
Lineart by Meredith Dillman

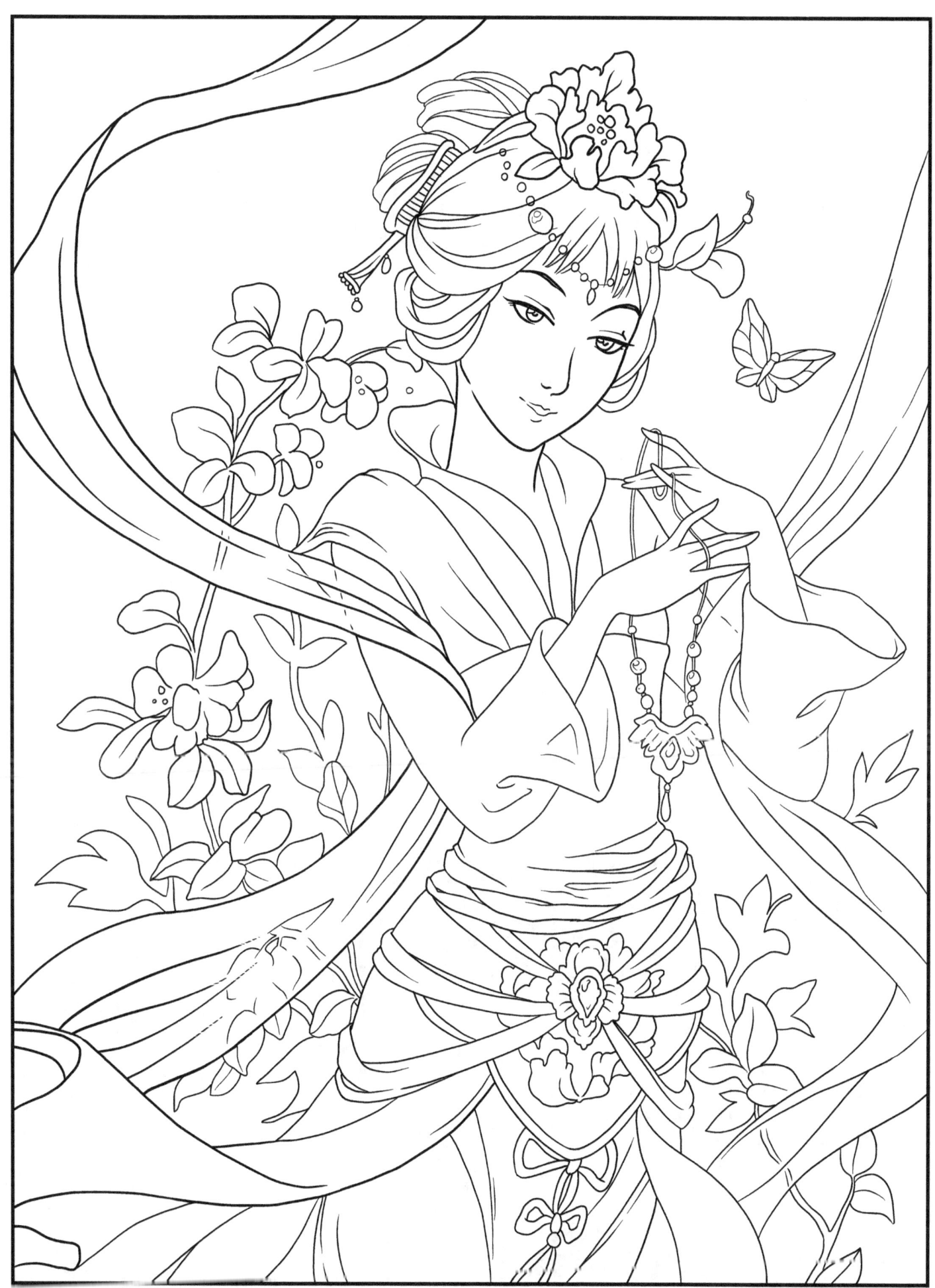

Previous Page: Jade
Lineart by Meredith Dillman

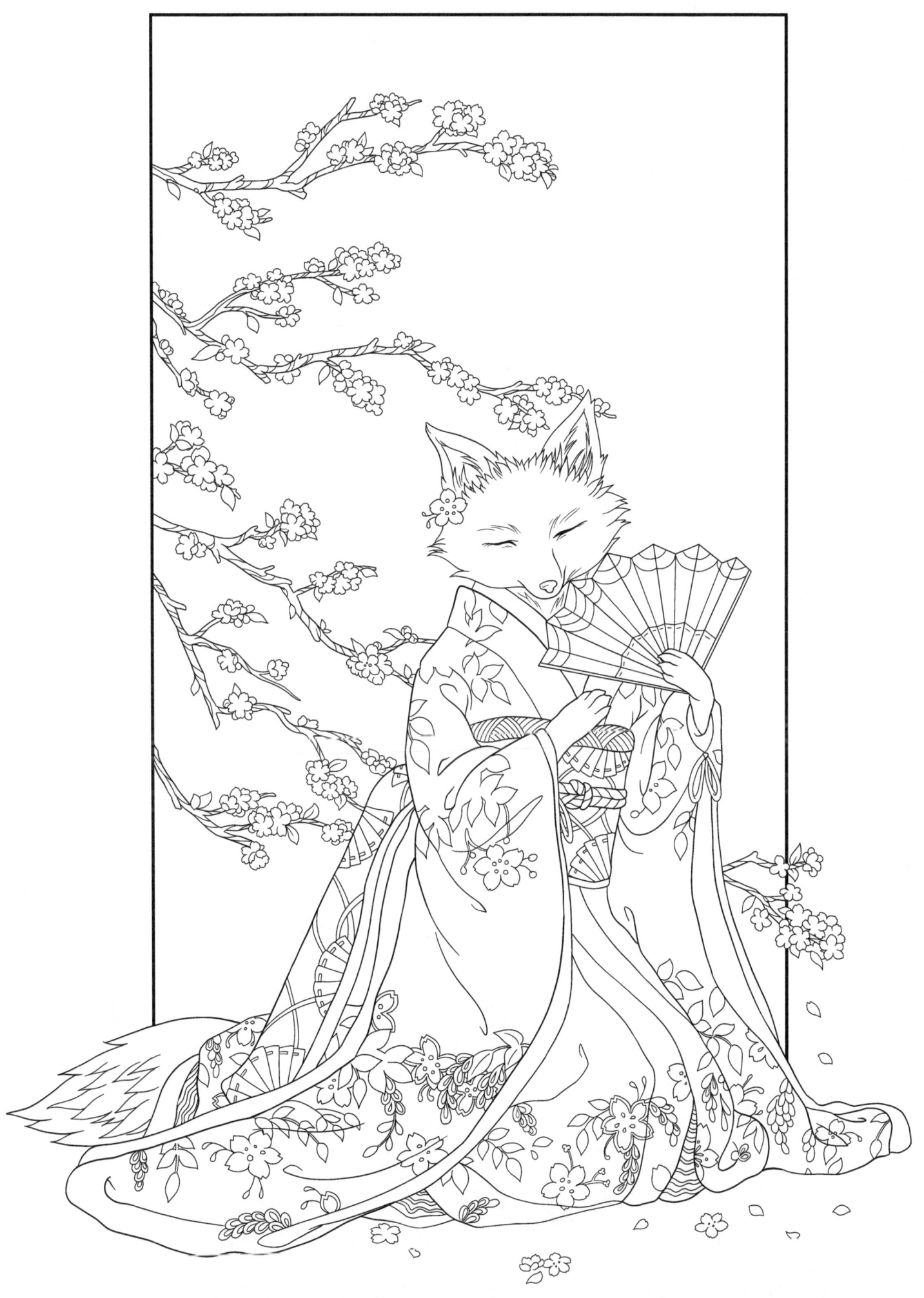

Previous Page: Haru (Spring)
Lineart by Meredith Dillman

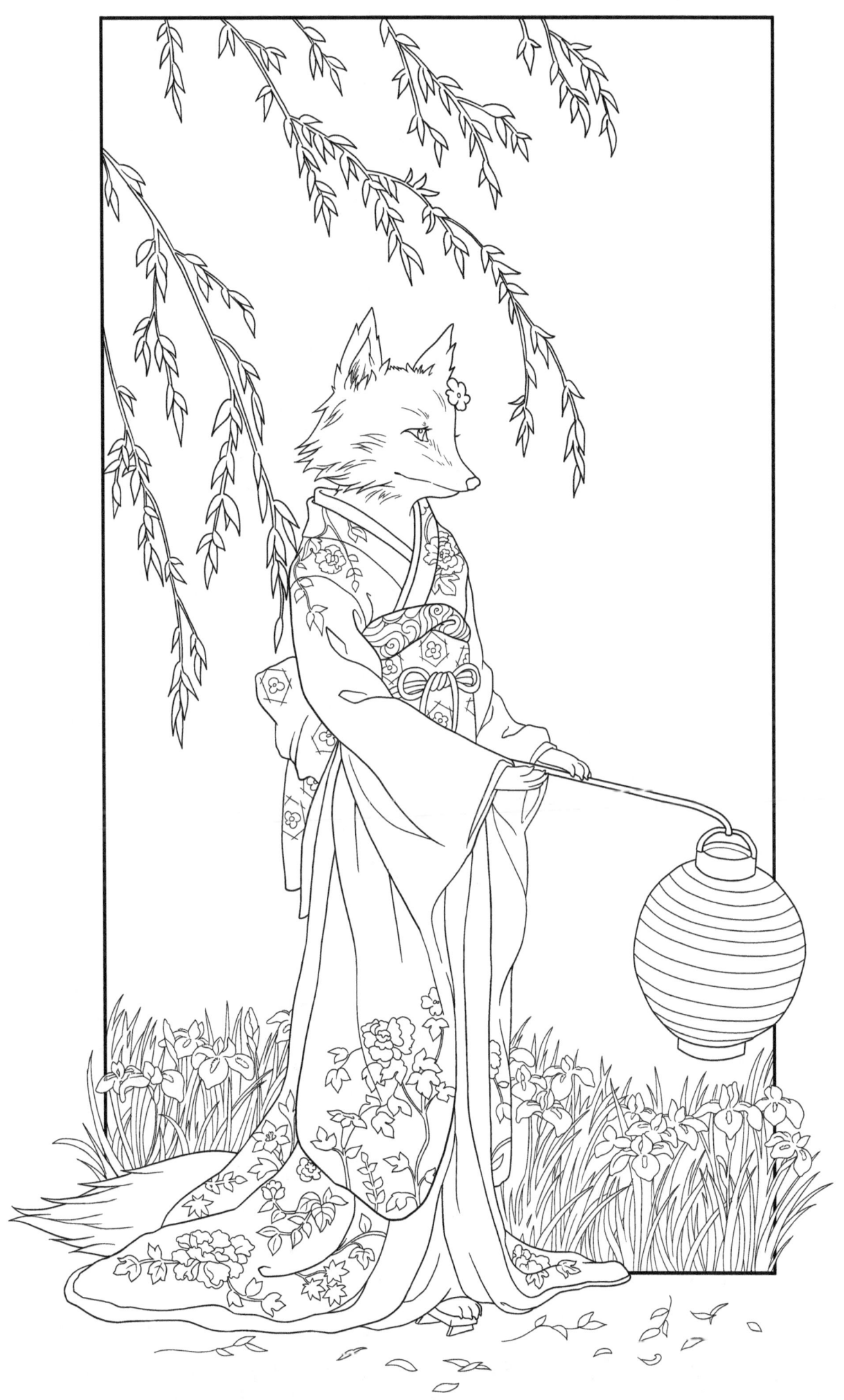

Previous Page: Natsu (Summer)
Lineart by Meredith Dillman

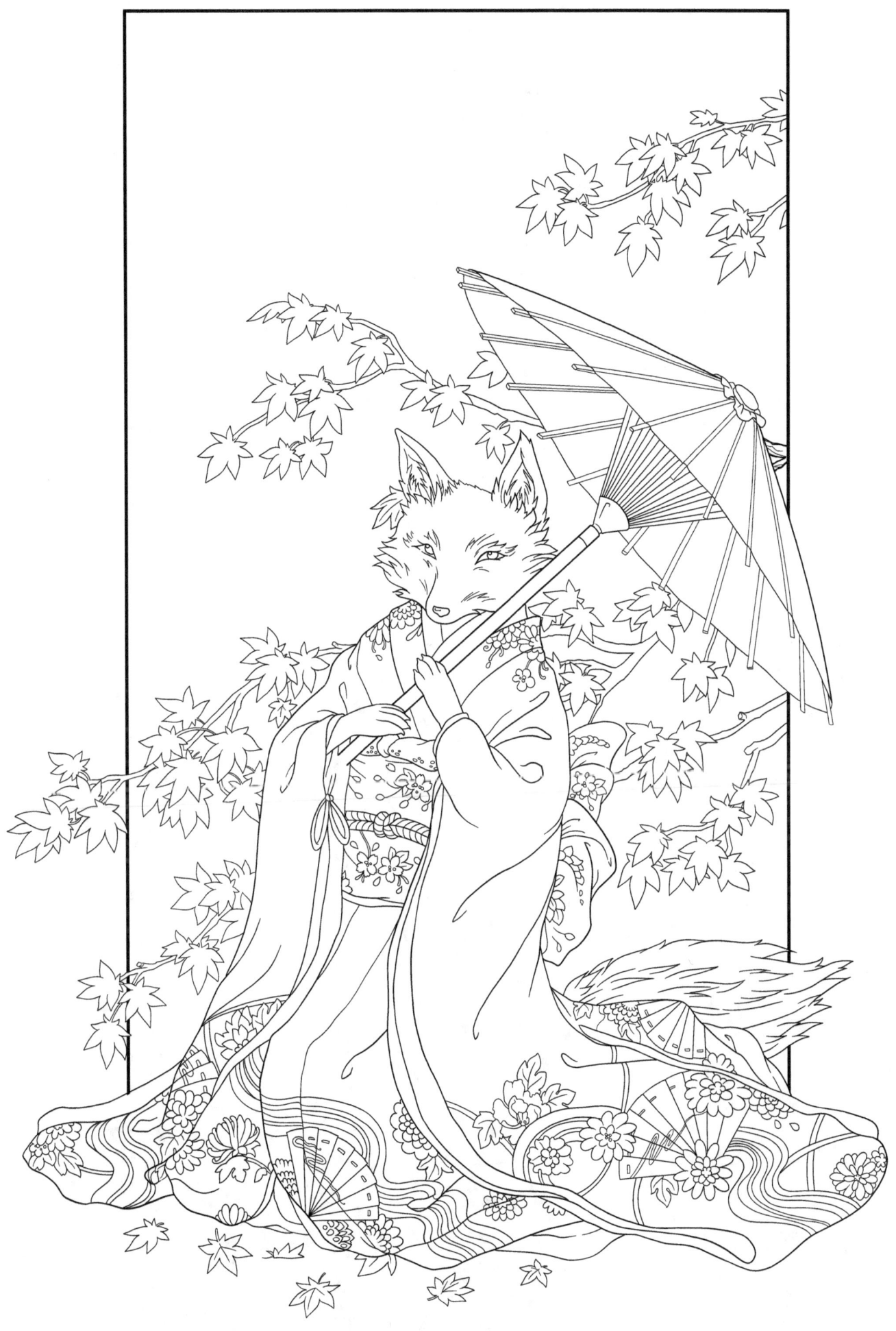

Previous Page: Aki (Autumn)
Lineart by Meredith Dillman

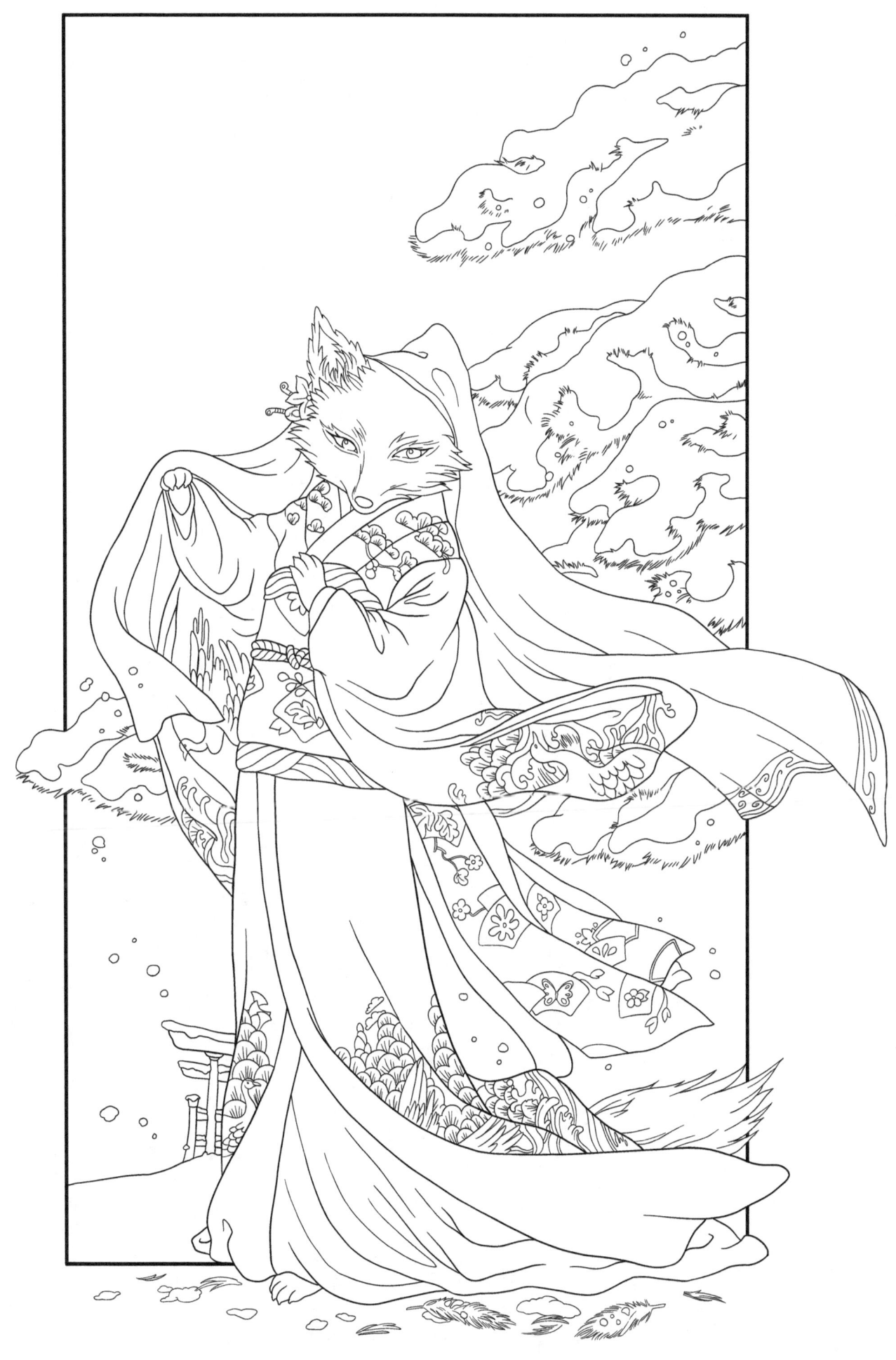

Previous Page: Yuki (Snow)
Lineart by Meredith Dillman

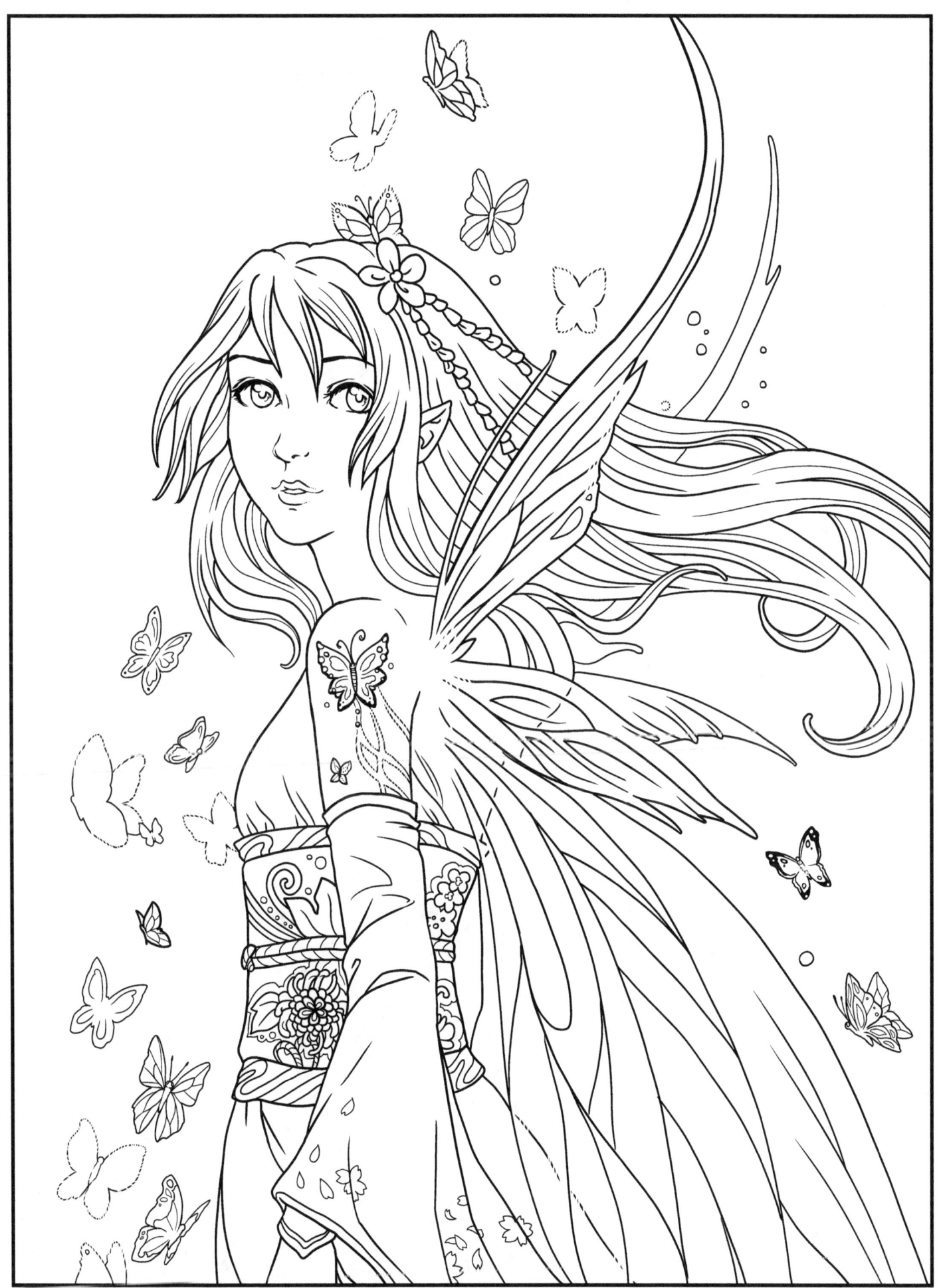

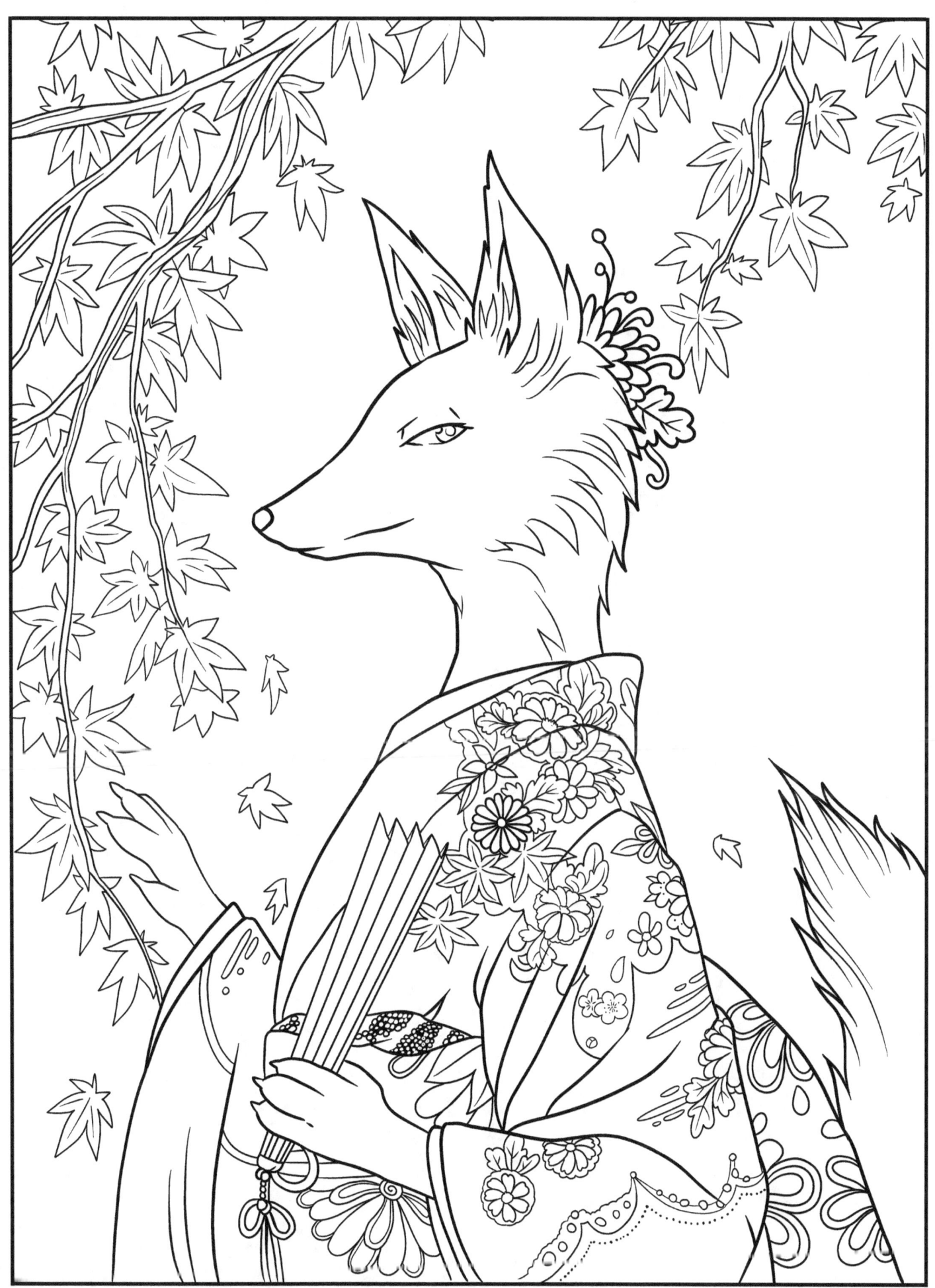

Previous Page: Maple Kitsune
Lineart by Meredith Dillman

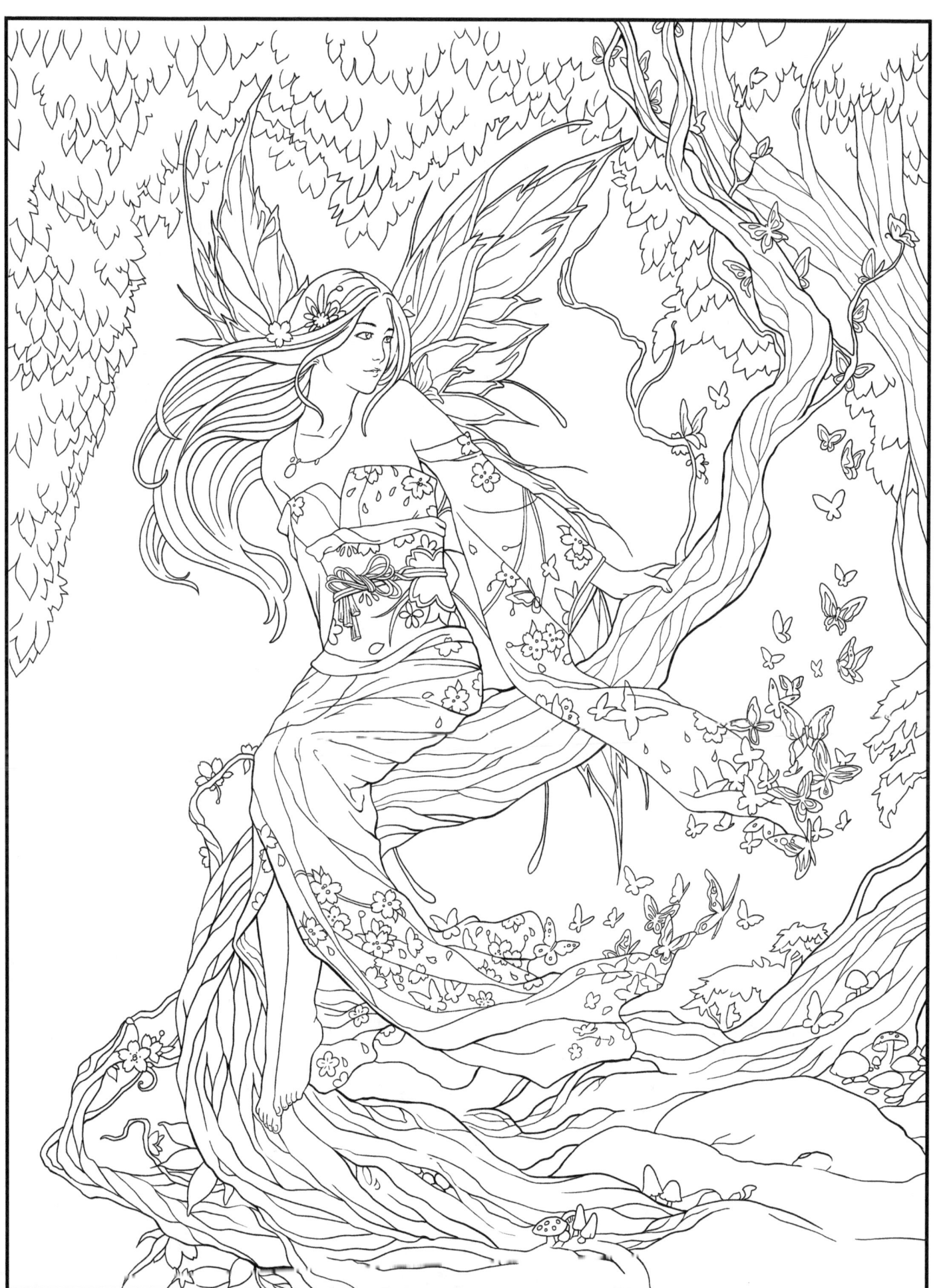

Previous Page: The Edge of Enchantment
Lineart by Meredith Dillman

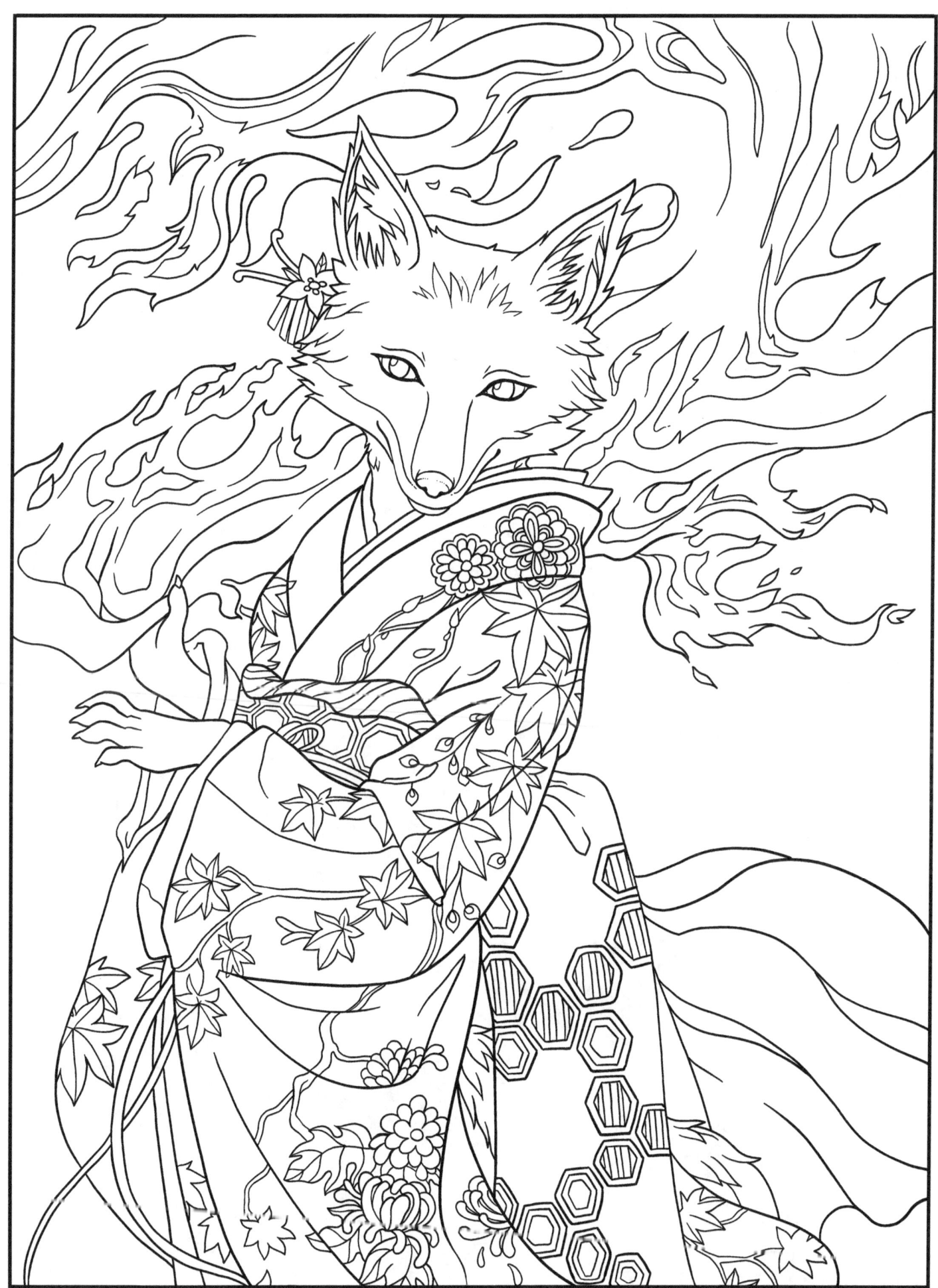

Previous Page: Foxfire
Lineart by Meredith Dillman

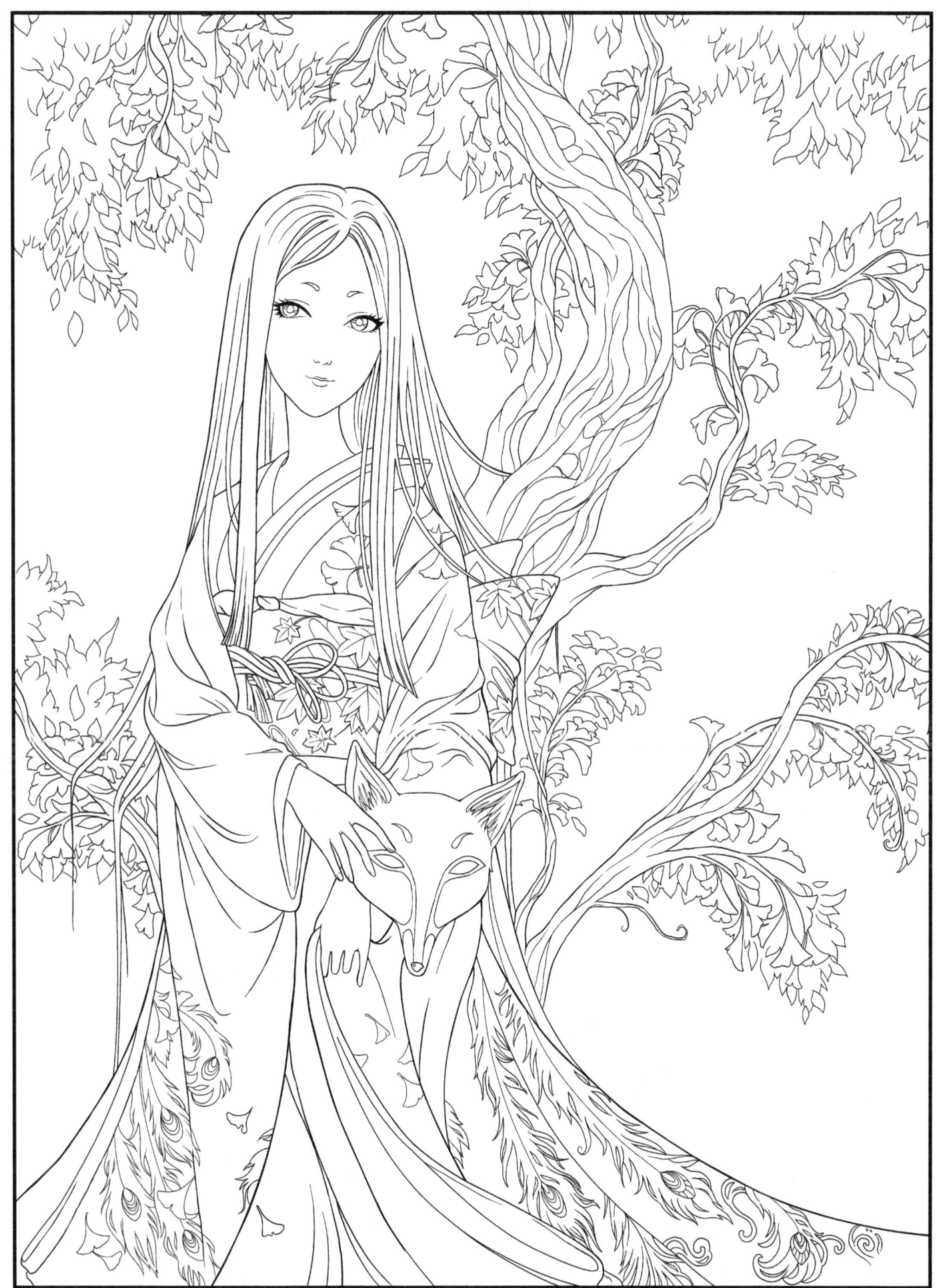

Previous Page: Spirit of the Ginkgo
Lineart by Meredith Dillman

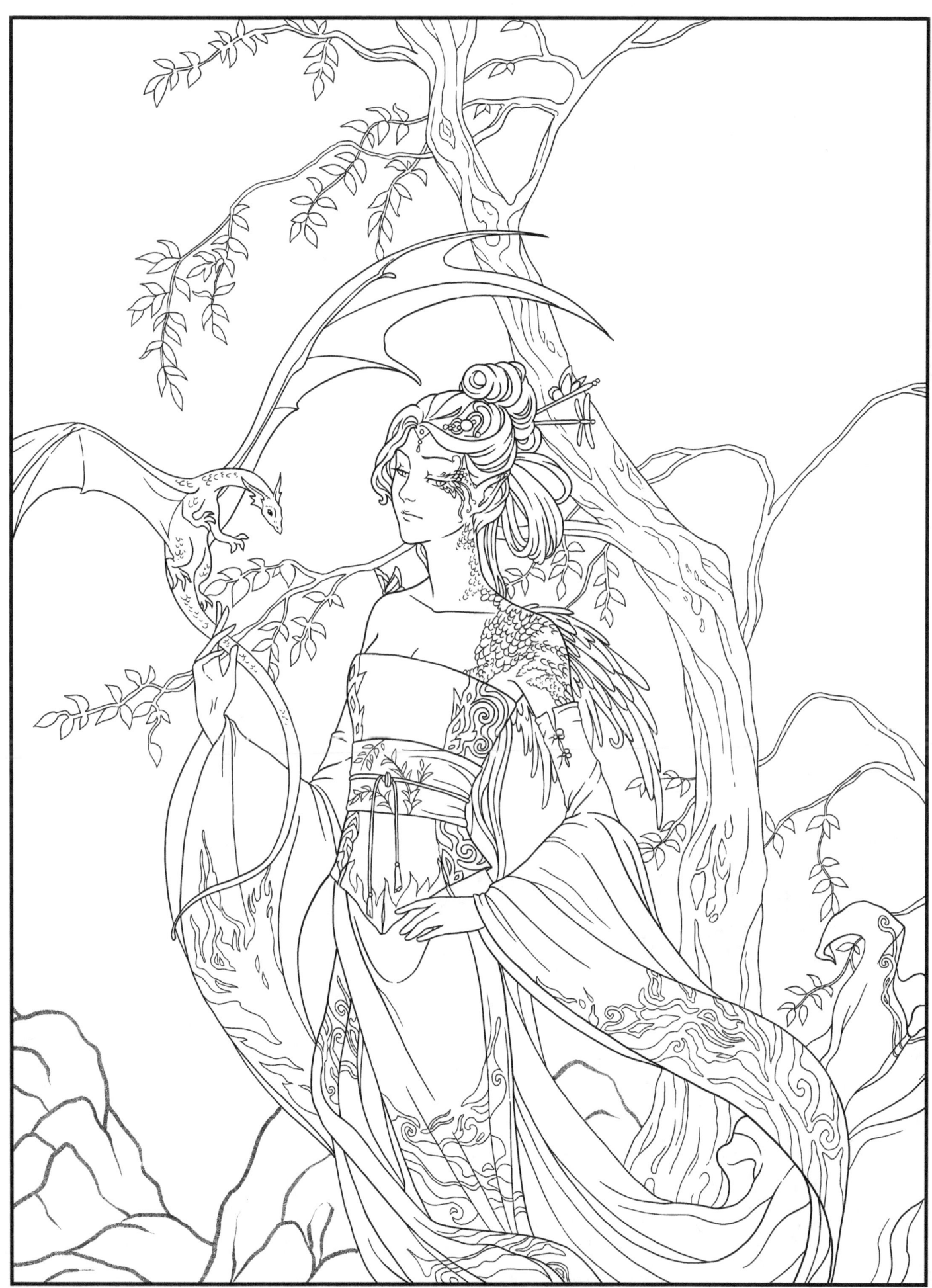

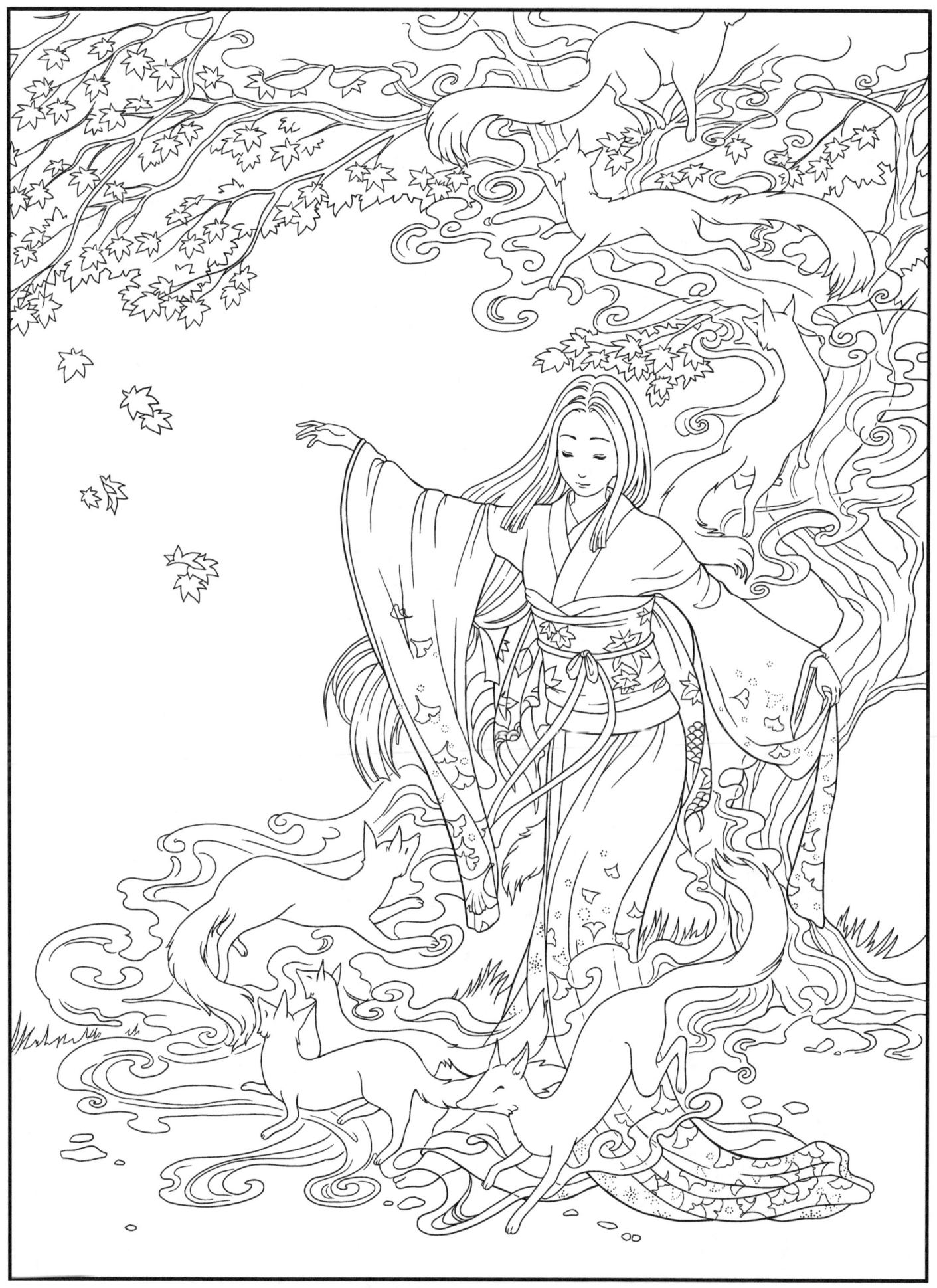

Previous Page: Kitsune Dance
Lineart by Meredith Dillman

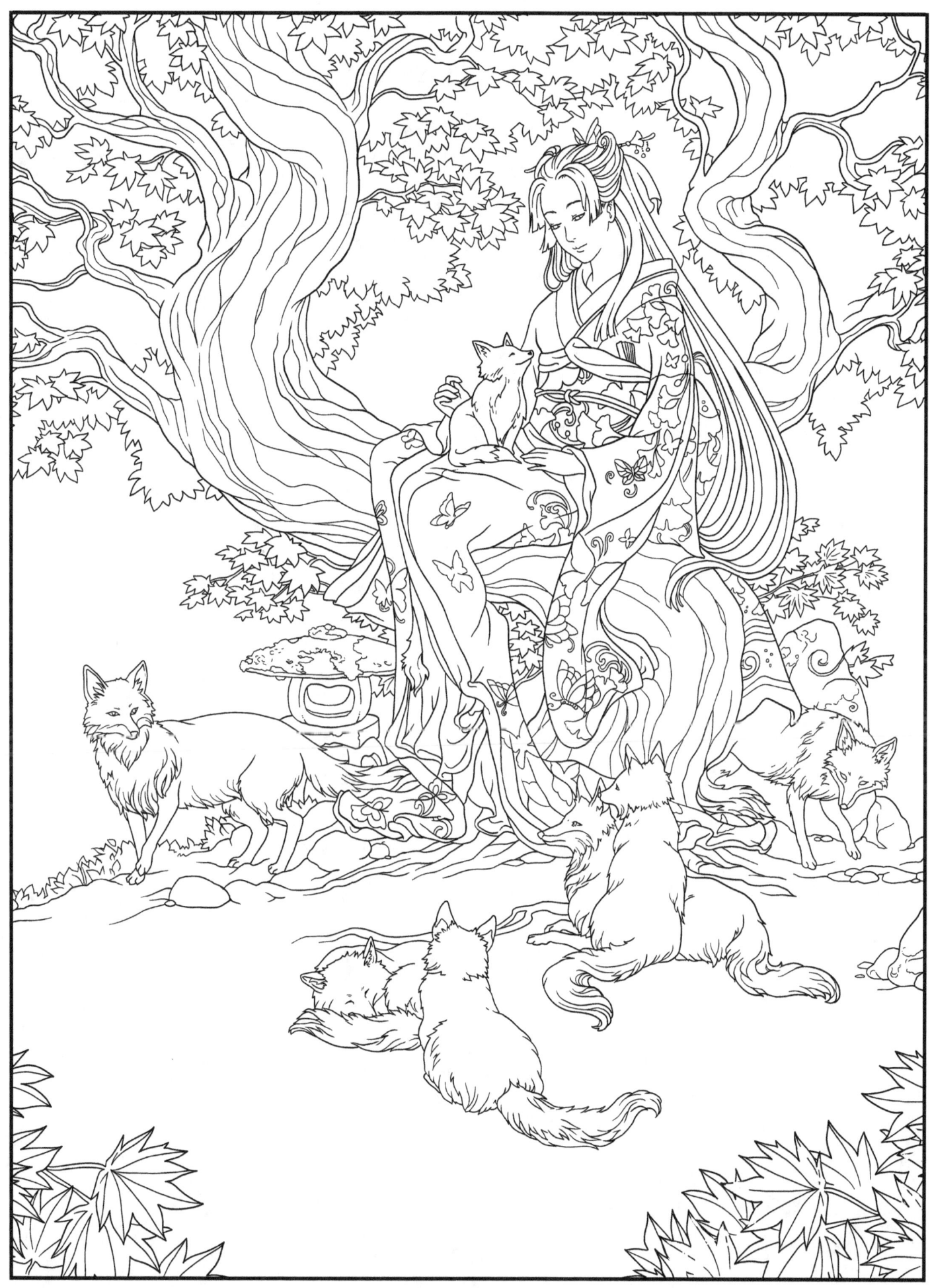

Previous Page: Kitsune Glen
Lineart by Meredith Dillman

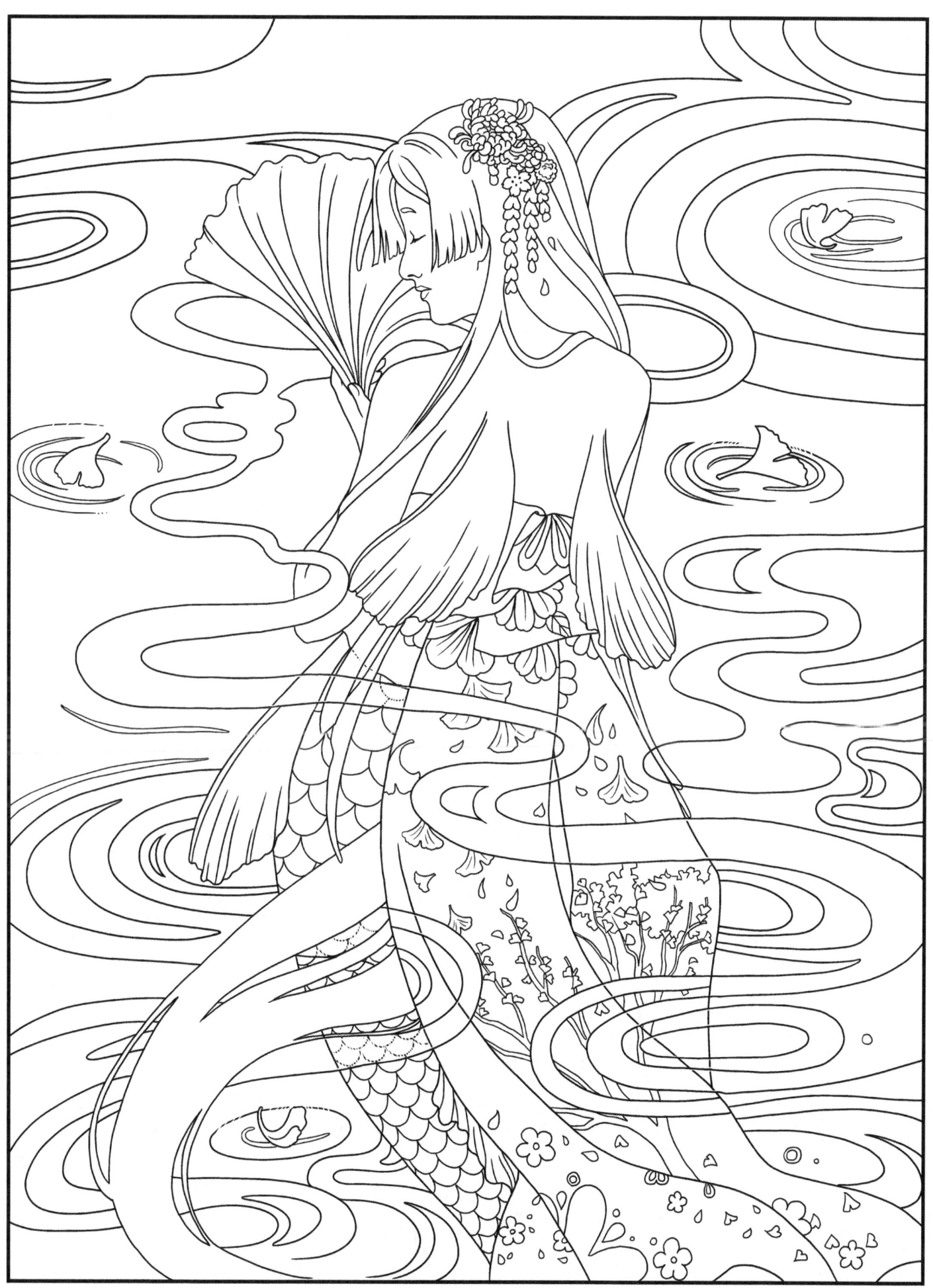

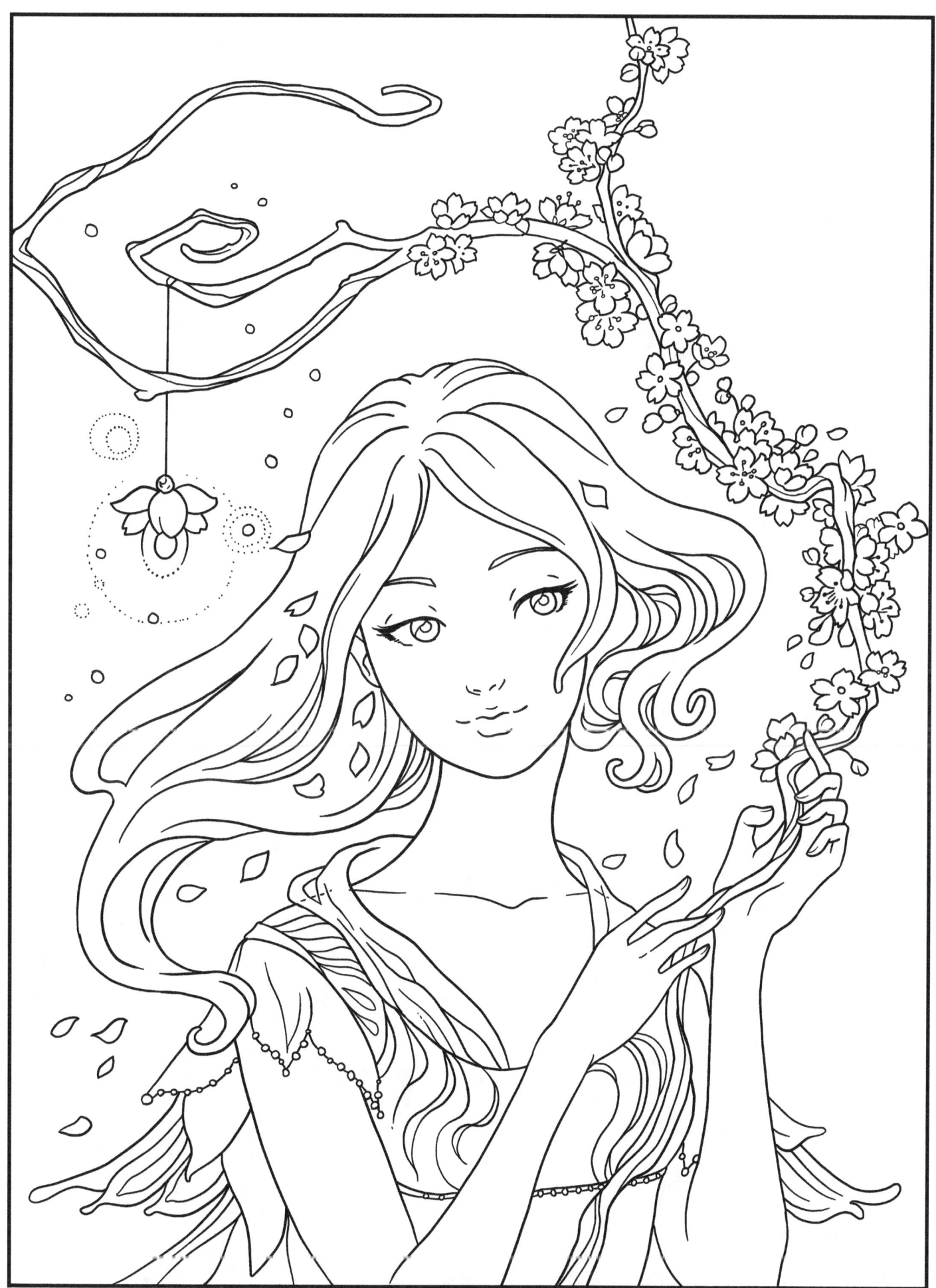

Previous Page: Sakura Breeze
Lineart by Meredith Dillman

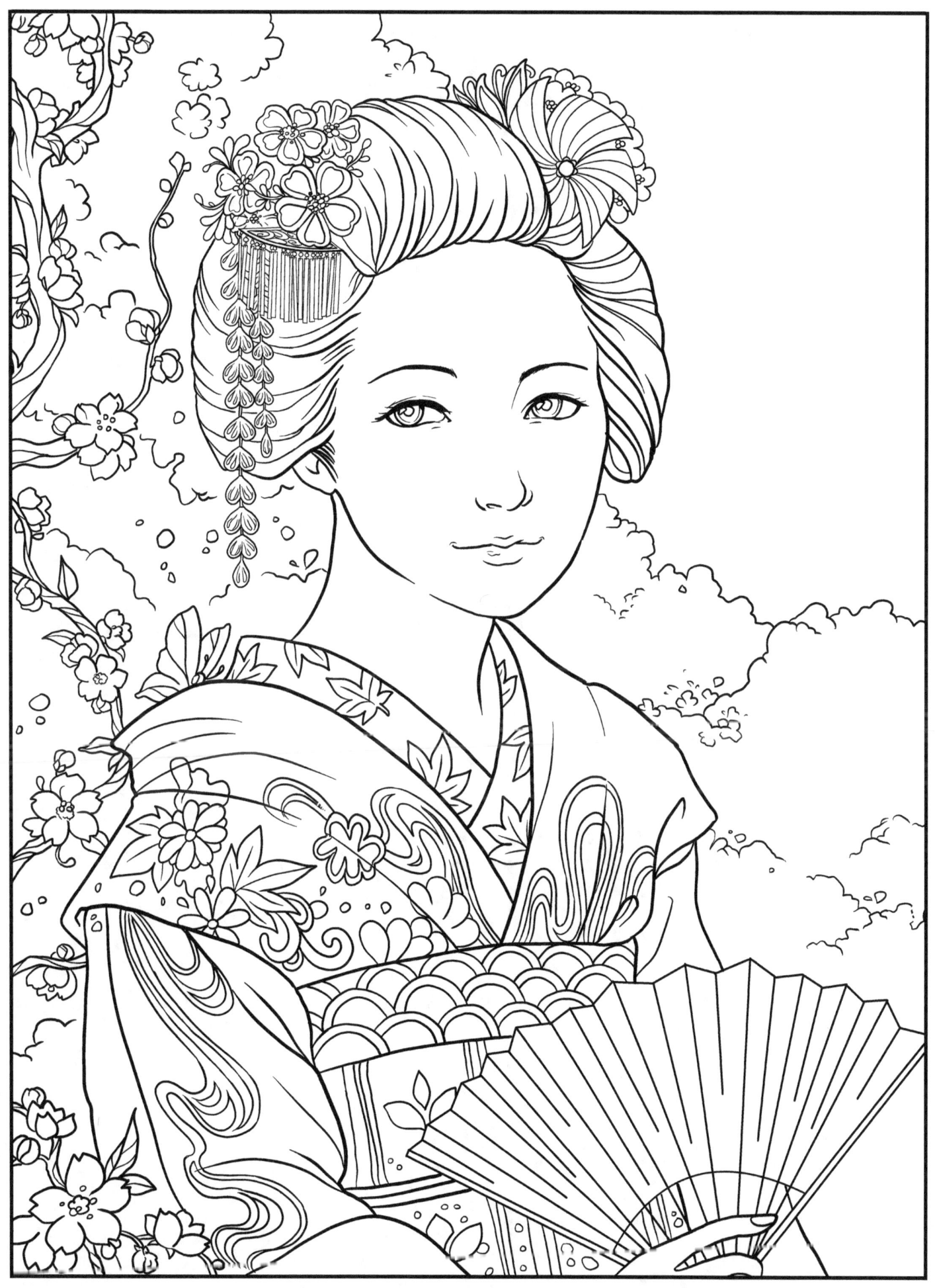

Previous Page: Maiko
Lineart by Meredith Dillman

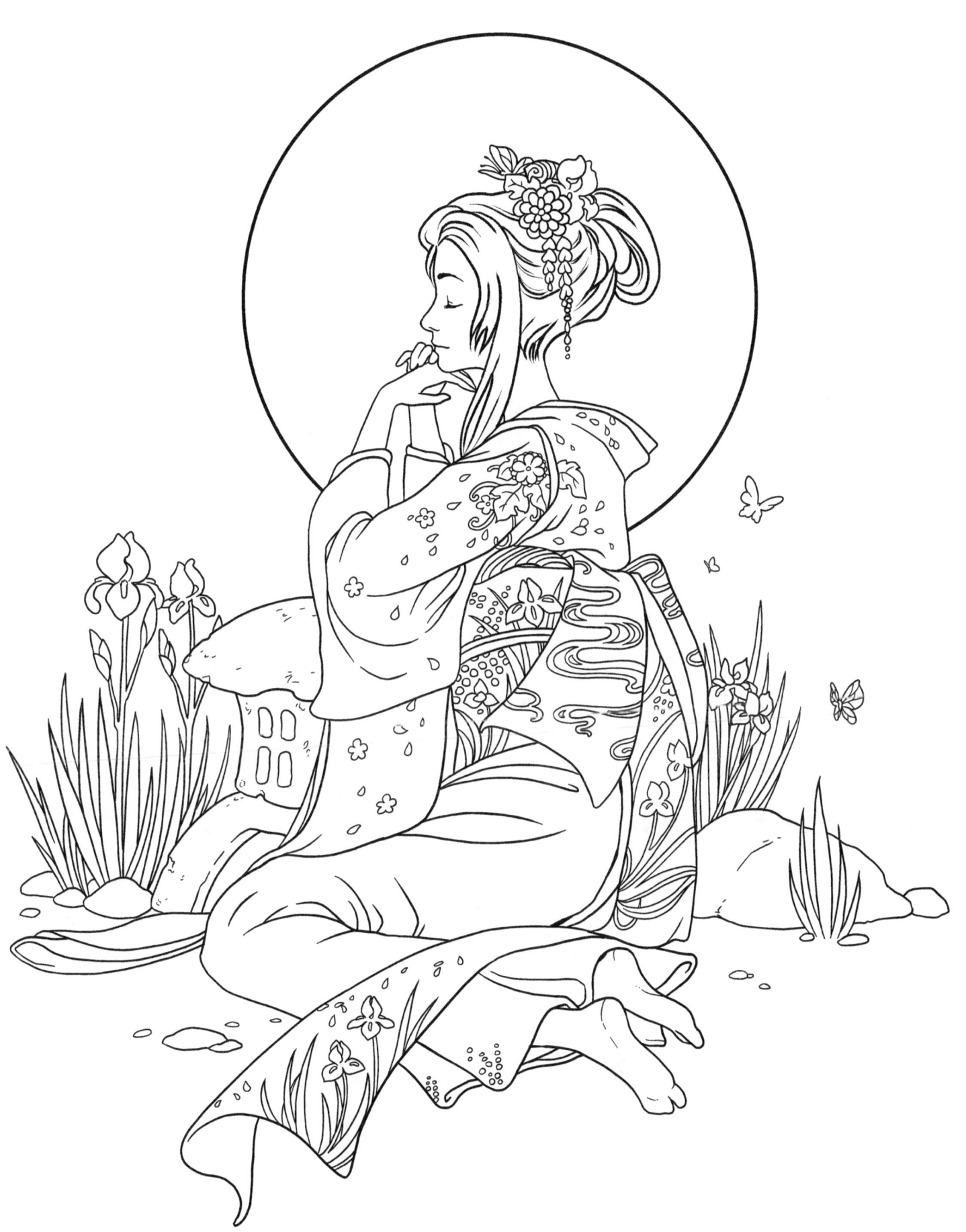

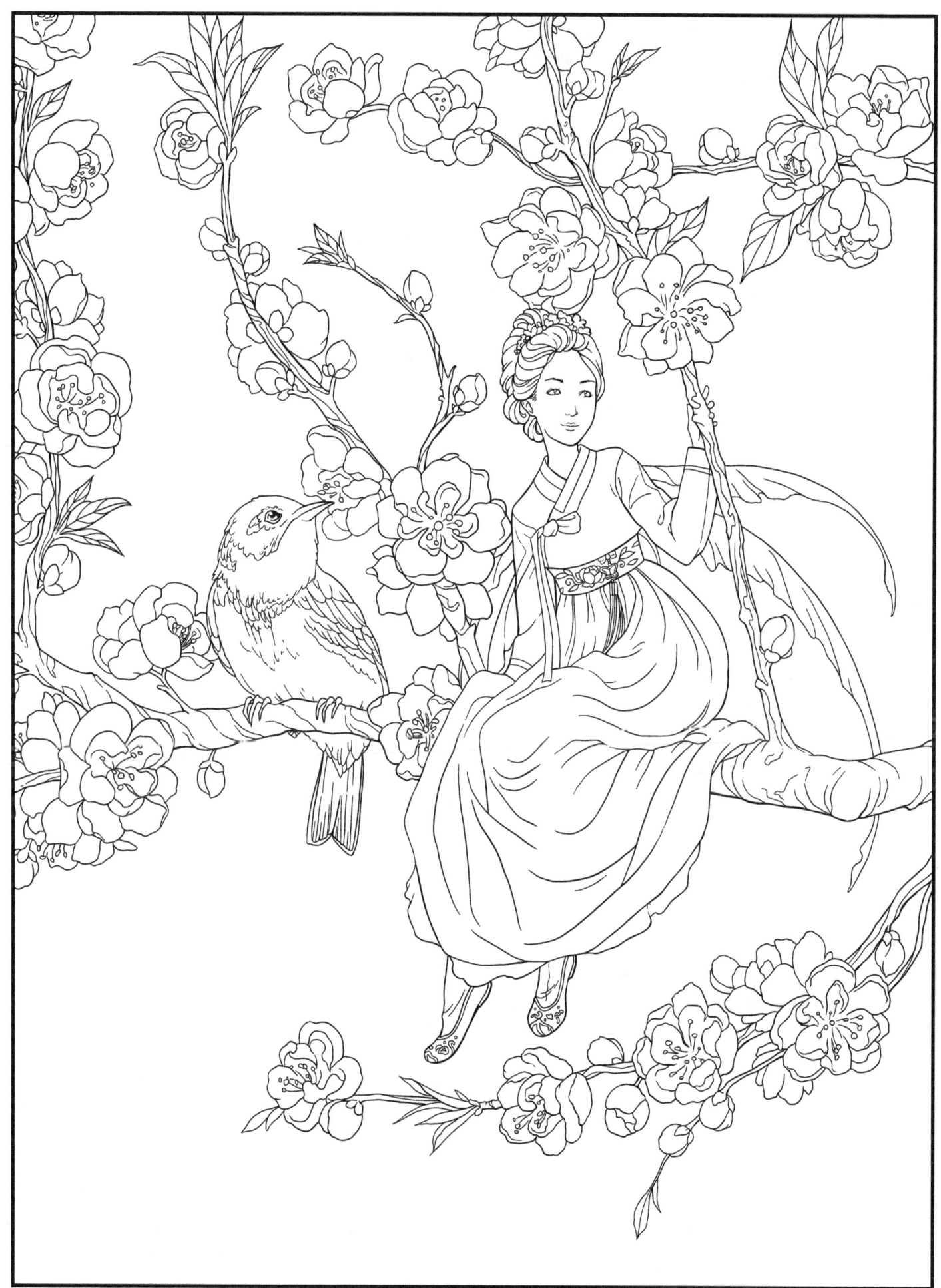

Previous Page: Peach Blossom
Lineart by Meredith Dillman

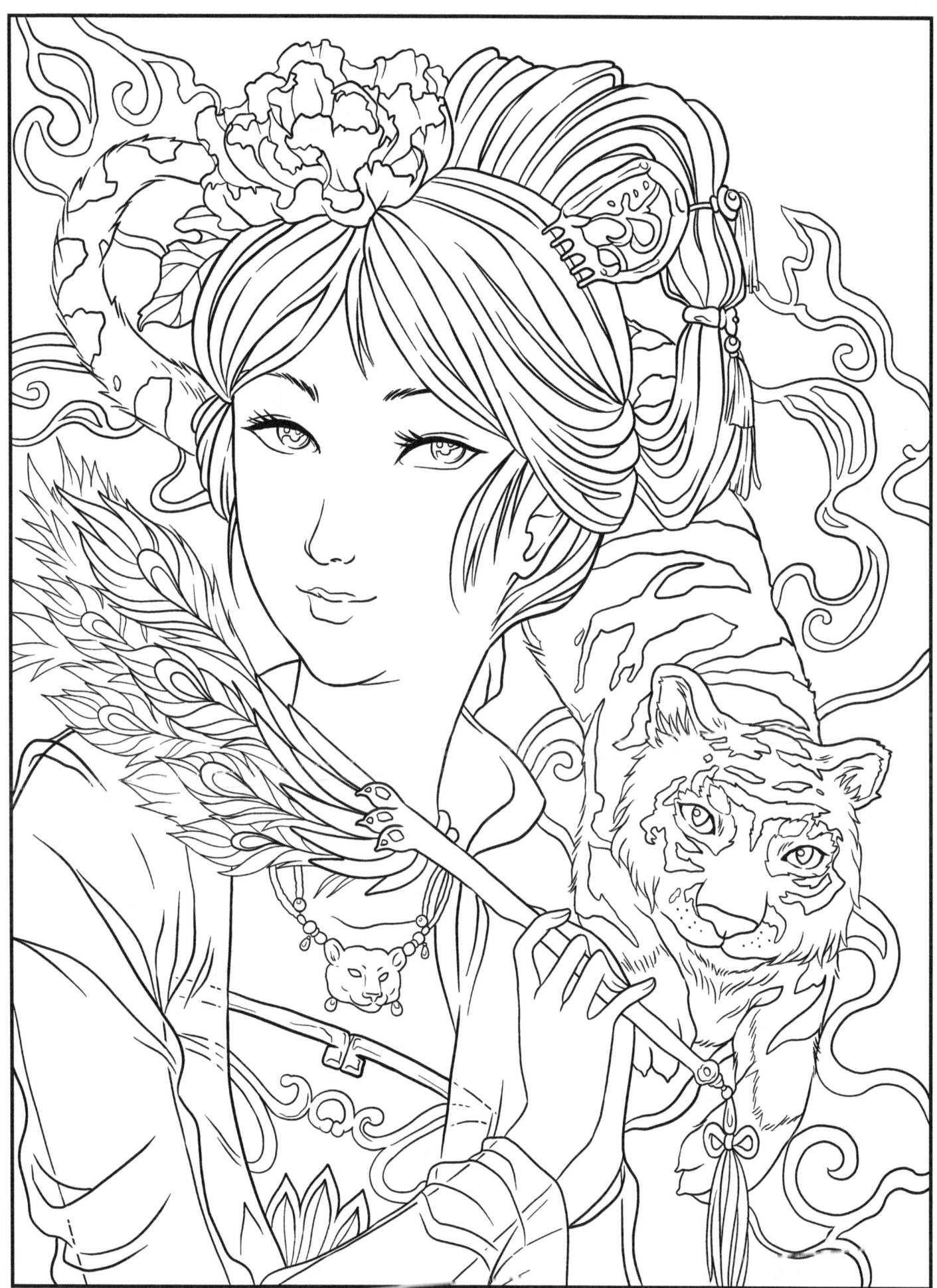

Previous Page: Chinese Zodiac - Tiger
Lineart by Meredith Dillman

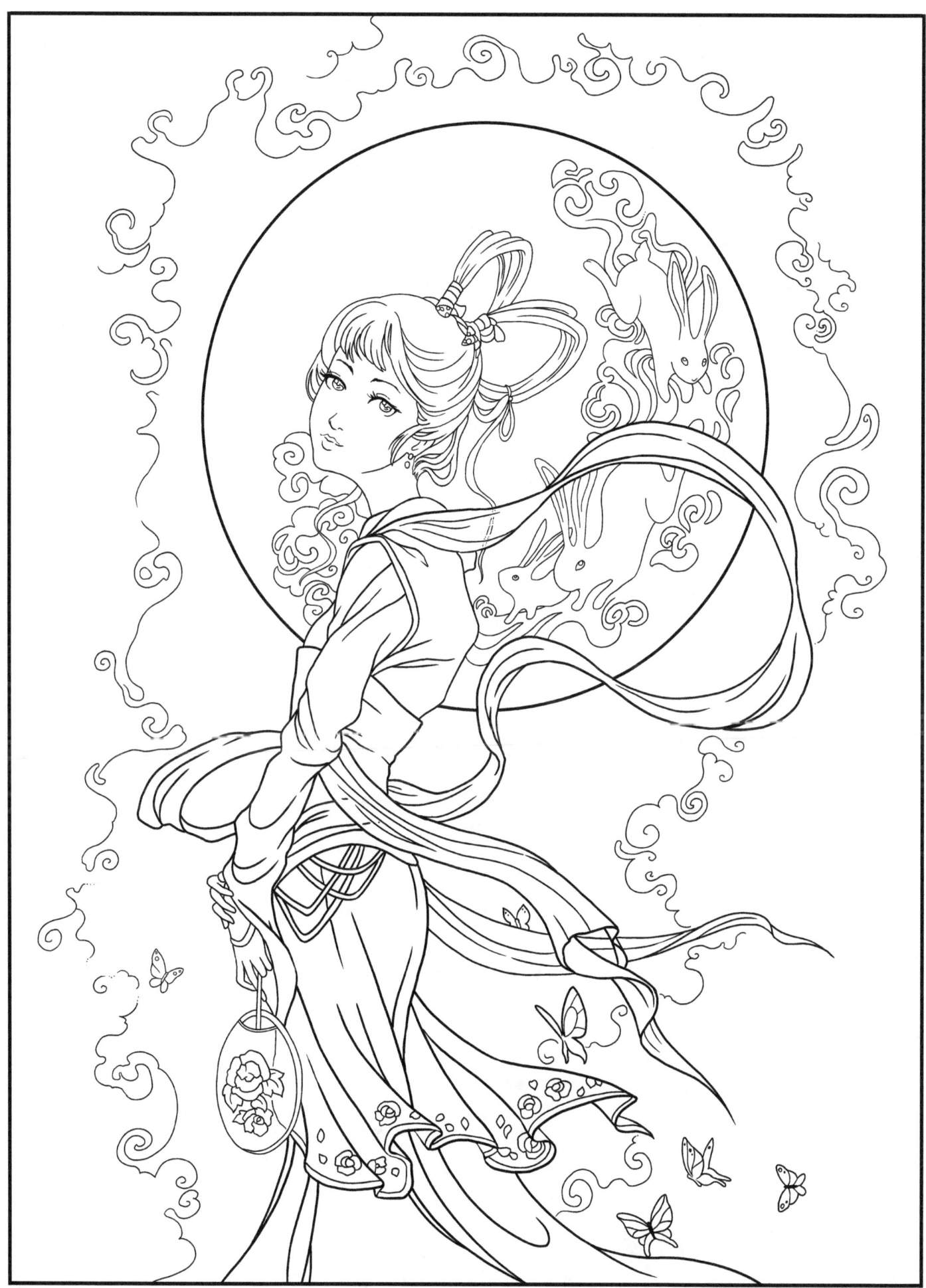

Previous Page: Chinese Zodiac – Rabbit
Lineart by Meredith Dillman

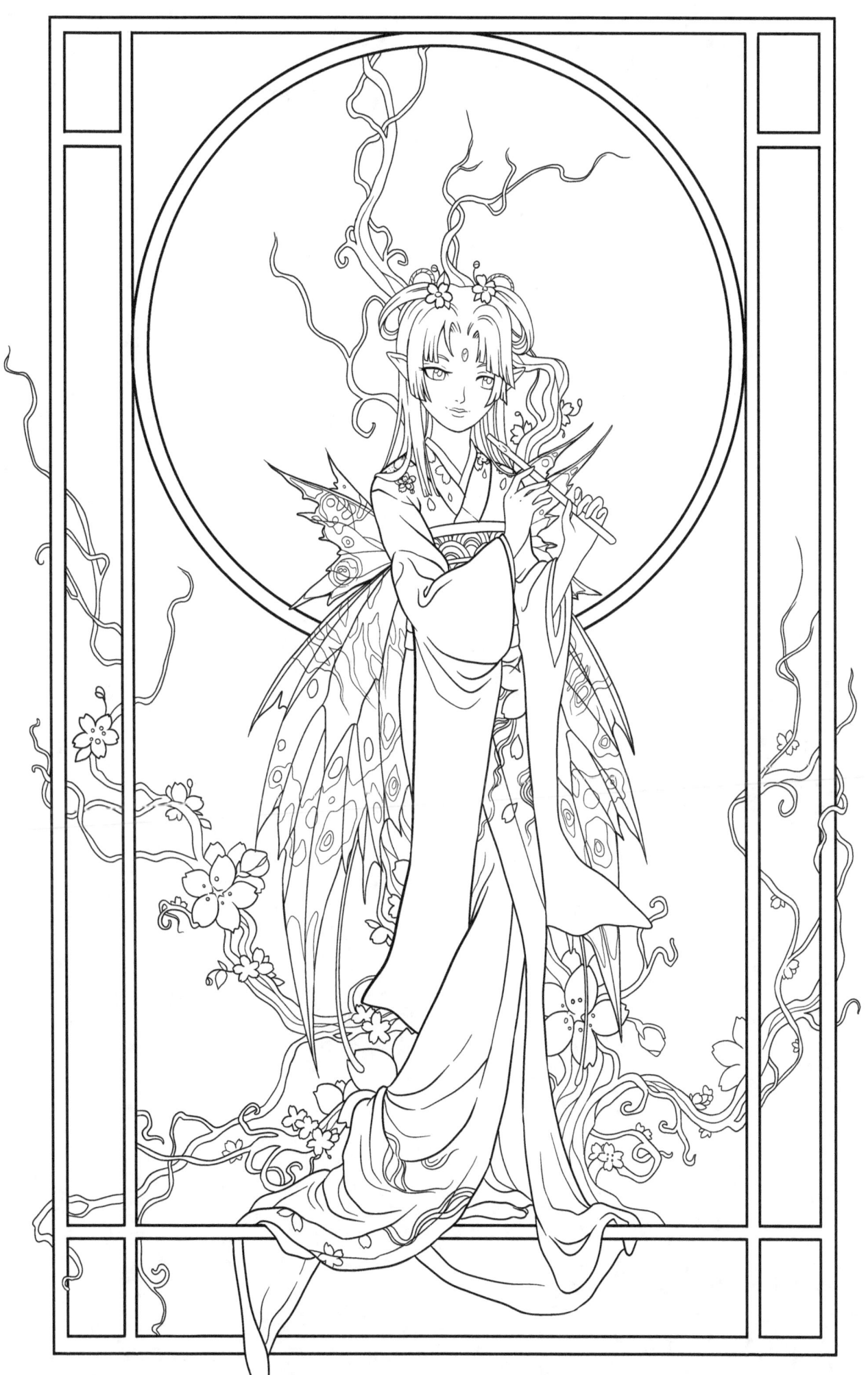

Previous Page: The Sweet Music of Spring
Lineart by Meredith Dillman

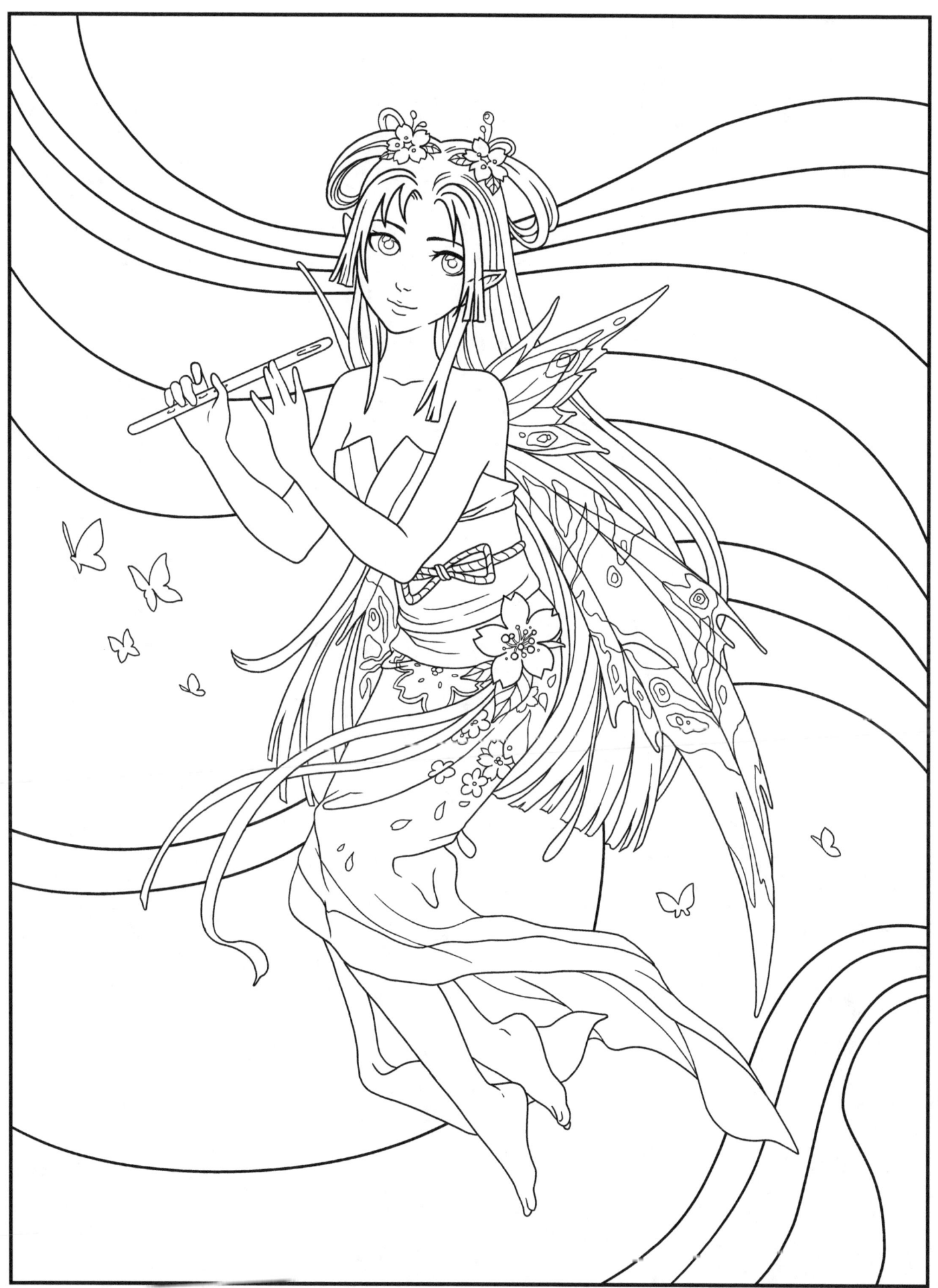

Previous Page: Little Kimono Fairy
Lineart by Meredith Dillman